The Most Dangerous

Philip Steele

KINGFISHER

First published 2013 by Kingfisher
an imprint of Macmillan Children's Books
a division of Macmillan Publishers Limited
20 New Wharf Road, London N1 9RR
Basingstoke and Oxford
Associated companies throughout the world
www.panmacmillan.com

Series editor: Polly Goodman
Literacy consultant: Hilary Horton

ISBN: 978-0-7534-3100-9
Copyright © Macmillan Publishers Ltd 2013

9 8 7 6 5 4 3 2 1
1TR/1012/WKT/UG/105MA

A CIP catalogue record for this book is available from the British Library.
Printed in China

Picture credits

The Publisher would like to thank the following for permission to reproduce their material.
Top = t; Bottom = b; Centre = c; Left = l; Right = r. Cover Shutterstock (SS)/djgis; cover t SS/Melinda Fawyer; c SS/Steshkin Yevgeniy; b Corbis/Mike Kireev/Demotix; 2l Getty/Hermann Erber/LOOK; 2cl SS/Steshkin Yevgeniy; 2c SS/Cheryl Ann Quigley; 2cr Photoshot/NHPA; 2r Getty/digital vision; 3l Corbis/Denis Scott; 3cl Corbis/Alberto Garcia; 3c FLPA/Frans Lanting; 3cr Photoshot/UPPA; 3r SS/bruno ismael da silva alves; 4 Getty/Stone; 5r Getty/Robert Mackinlay/Peter Arnold; 5bl Getty/ Photographer's Choice; 6 Getty/Imagesource; 7 Corbis/Bohemian Nomad Picturemakers; 8 Corbis/Naturfoto Honal; 9 Photoshot/NHPA; 10 Corbis/Denis Scott; 11cl Getty/OSF; 11br FLPA/Norbert Wu; 12 Getty/Jerry Young/ DK; 13ctl KF Archive (KF); 13ctr SS/Steve Collender; 13cbl Nature/Tony Phelps; 13cbr KF; 13br Corbis/ Imagemore co.; 14bl SS/Ratikova; 15t SS/Ilya Andriyanov; 15b Corbis/Pierre Holtz/Reuters; 16 Corbis/Joe McDonald; 17ctl SS/Gilmanshin ; 17ctr KF; 17cbl Nature/Robert Valentic; 17cbr Nature/Robert Valentic; 17b Alamy/A&J Visage; 18 FLPA/Frans Lanting; 19t KF; 19b SS/Dr J. Beller; 20 SS/Karl W.; 21tr SS/Cheryl Ann Quigley; 21br Getty/James Balog/Stone; 22 SS/Natursports; 23tr Corbis/Hugh Sitton; 23br Corbis/ Denis Kunkel; 24cl Getty/Vetta; 24b KF; 25 Getty/AFP; 26cl SS/Mark Yarchoan; 26b Photoshot/Moodboard; 27 Corbis/Alberto Garcia; 28tl SS/Steshkin Yevgeniy; 28b Corbis/Richard H. Cohen; 29 Getty/The Image Bank; 30 Photoshot/Firoz Ahmed/Drik/Majority World; 31t Photoshot/UPPA; 31b KF; 32 Getty/LOOK; 33 Getty/All Canada Photos; 34 SS/bruno ismael da silva alves; 35 Corbis/Andry Prasetyo/Reuters; 36 SS/ Germanskydiver; 37tr Getty/Hermann Erber/LOOK; 37br Corbis/Mike Kireev/Demotix; 38 Rex Features/ Anthony Upton; 39t Corbis/Transtock; 39b Corbis/CSPA/NewSport; 40 Corbis/Derek M. Allan/Travel Ink; 41 Corbis/Marcelo Hernanadez/dpa; 42tl Getty/Stone; 42b Alamy/Patrick Forget/Sagaphoto; 43tr Alamy/ David Osborn; 44tl Getty/digital vision; 44b SS/EpicStockMedia; 45tr Getty/Stone; 45cr Getty/Photolibrary; 46l Getty/Hermann Erber/LOOK; 46cl SS/Steshkin Yevgeniy; 46c SS/Cheryl Ann Quigley; 46cr Photoshot/ NHPA; 46r Getty/digital vision; 47l Corbis/Denis Scott; 47cl Corbis/Alberto Garcia; 47c FLPA/Frans Lanting; 47cr Photoshot/UPPA; 47r SS/bruno ismael da silva alves.

Contents

A lifetime of danger	4
The body's defences	6
Don't eat these!	8
Ocean killers	10
Spiders and scorpions	12
Insect danger	14
Deadly snakes	16
Croc attack!	18
Tooth, tusk and claw	20
Spreaders of disease	22
Quakes and waves	24
Volcano blast	26
Storm and wind	28
Flood warning	30
Snow and ice	32
The big heat	34
Extreme sports	36
Daredevils	38
Dangerous work	40
Emergency!	42
Living with danger	44
Glossary	46
Index	48

A lifetime of danger

Just staying alive can be dangerous. We face all kinds of dangers during our lifetime. As young children we learn to keep away from hot ovens or fierce dogs. We are taught how to play football or cycle without being injured. We soon find out how to keep ourselves safe.

At some time in our lives, we may be at risk from illnesses or from accidents or sporting injuries. More unusual dangers might include poisoning by plants or terrifying attacks by wild animals. We may find ourselves at risk from large natural disasters such as floods or earthquakes.

A tiger bares its teeth and snarls. This powerful big cat roams the forests of Asia.

Many of us enjoy some risk. Mountain climbers or explorers welcome adventurous challenges. Others may prefer to get their thrills from exciting films, books or computer games.

People can be clever and brave. They learn how to protect their bodies from harm. They try to protect other people, too, and save lives. They meet dangerous challenges and learn from their experiences.

Climbing is dangerous but exciting.

Warning signs tell us if there is danger ahead.

The body's defences

Our bodies have many natural ways of protecting themselves from harm. If we hurt ourselves, our **nerves** pick up the danger signals at once. They send a message to the brain. We feel the pain and take action to stop it.

Eyelashes and eyelids shield our eyes from grit. Nails protect our fingertips and toes. Skin and the **vessels** that carry blood around our body help to control our temperature. This makes it less likely that we will die from extreme cold or heat.

Adrenalin helps this cowboy handle a dangerous situation.

When we are faced by danger, we need super powers! A **gland** in our body produces adrenalin. This substance pumps extra oxygen into our blood and makes our heart speed up. It stiffens the muscles. It helps us to concentrate, so that we can fight – or run away fast!

Our protection against illnesses and wounds is called the immune system. Its weapons include white blood cells, which destroy **germs**. Our body can repair itself and recover from grazes, sprains or even broken bones.

Rapid response
When we are in trouble, our nervous system can send messages to and from the brain at speeds of 100 metres per second!

Don't eat these!

Beware belladonna, or deadly nightshade – it has highly poisonous berries and leaves.

We eat many different plants, but some plants are dangerous. This is because they have defences to keep away people and animals. Sharp thorns can tear our skin and stinging hairs can cause a painful rash. The juices of some plants, such as euphorbias, can blister the skin or damage the eyes.

The biggest risk is from plants that have berries, leaves, roots or seeds that are poisonous to eat. They are often mistaken for harmless plants. People may become sick or even die if they eat them. Extremely dangerous plants include hemlock, foxglove and monkshood.

Some fungi, such as mushrooms, are popular foods, but other fungi are deadly. The one that kills the most people is called the deathcap. Its poison causes vomiting and extreme pain, as it attacks the liver and kidneys. It is pale green or yellowish. Young ones are round, but the head grows and flattens to about 5 to 15 centimetres across. People can mistake the deathcap for other fungi that are safe to eat.

A dish of death
In 1534 one of the most powerful men in the world, Pope Clement VII, died after eating a deathcap mushroom. Was it an accident? Many people believe he was killed by a poisoner.

The fatal deathcap mushroom grows mostly in woodlands in Europe.

DO NOT EAT!
Never eat any wild plants, berries or fungi without checking with an adult first.

Ocean killers

Very few animals hunt humans, but some will attack people if they are in danger themselves. Animals are often most fierce when they are protecting their young.

One of the most feared animals is the great white shark. It hunts in the warm waters of the Atlantic, Pacific and Indian oceans. This fish can grow up to six metres long. It has a keen sense of smell, and its snout is packed with about 300 sharp teeth.

Blood in the sea
About 100 shark attacks on humans happen each year, and one-third of these are made by great white sharks.

Sharks sometimes attack swimmers, when they confuse them with their food. These attacks are rare. Each year, more people are killed by toasters than by sharks!

Many jellyfish deliver a painful sting from their tentacles. The most dangerous ones live in the Indian and Pacific oceans. They are known as box jellies, marine stingers or sea wasps. They produce powerful

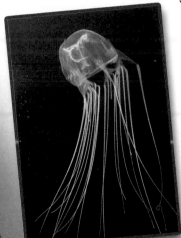

venom, which they use to kill their **prey**. A really bad sting can kill a human if it is not treated. It may take just a few minutes for the venom to stop the heart working.

The stinging tentacles of the sea wasp can trail for three metres.

Beach safety can save lives. Signs such as this one warn bathers about jellyfish.

Spiders and scorpions

They are only small, but the way spiders and scorpions scuttle and hide in dark corners often gives us a scare.

Spiders have mouthparts that end in fangs. These inject venom to help kill prey, or to protect the spider if it is attacked. The most powerful spider venom can make you feel dizzy, sick and stiff, with blurred vision. It can cause painful blisters and even kill a person.

The most venomous spiders are found in Central and South American rainforests. They are called wandering or armed spiders. Their scientific name is *Phoneutria*, which means murderer! *Phoneutria* venom affects the nerves and muscles, and makes it hard to breathe.

Phoneutria spiders like to hide in bunches of bananas. They have long legs and extremely venomous fangs.

Don't let them bite!

There are about 38,000 **species** of spiders, but only 200 or so can hurt people. In North America watch out for black widow and brown recluse spiders. In Australia many funnel-web spiders can give a very nasty bite. In Africa beware of six-eyed sand spiders.

Black widow

Brown recluse spider

Six-eyed sand spider

Funnel-web spider

Scorpions have two big pincers and a raised, curved tail with a sting on the end that delivers a powerful venom. The most dangerous scorpion lives in North Africa and the Middle East. It is called the deathstalker. Its sting can be very painful indeed.

The curved tail of the deathstalker ends in a sharp needle that injects venom.

Insect danger

There are about a million insect species. Wasps, hornets and bees can all give a painful sting. If you upset a wasps' nest or a beehive, the insects may attack you in self-defence. Bees use 22 muscles to deliver just one jab. Their sting is made up of three **barbed** daggers, which deliver venom.

Getting stung in the mouth or throat is very dangerous, so be careful if a wasp is after your sandwiches! Stings are especially dangerous to people who are **allergic** to the venom.

Sting protection
Beekeepers wear special clothing to protect the body. People keep bees because they give us honey and help plants make fruit.

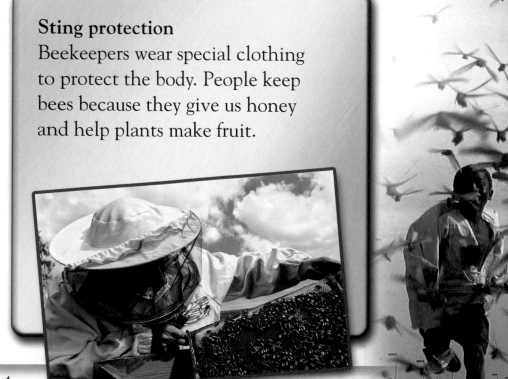

A wasp's sharp stinger is at the end of its tail.

The desert locust, which lives in Africa and Asia, forms great **swarms** that darken the sky. Locusts never bite or sting, but they are dangerous because they eat every plant in sight, including crops. Locusts strip the land bare, leaving people and animals with nothing to eat and at risk of **starvation**.

A single locust swarm can cover a vast area, with 40 to 80 million insects per square kilometre.

Deadly snakes

Some snakes are deadly because their bite is venomous. Others are dangerous because they coil their bodies around their prey. These are called constrictors.

About a quarter of the world's snakes produce venom. In warm lands where many of these snakes live, thousands of people die of bites each year.

Scientists have learned how to deal with snakebites. They take the venom from captured snakes and inject a tiny amount of it into another animal. The animal's immune system reacts against the venom, producing **chemicals** to protect itself. Scientists collect the chemicals to make **antivenoms**, which can save a life. Unfortunately, many snakebites occur in remote country areas, without easy access to doctors or hospitals.

A venomous snake shows its fangs.

The most snake bites
The most dangerous country for snakebites is Sri Lanka. On average, about 800 people are killed there every year.

Poisonous snakes

Black mamba: the longest venomous snake in Africa

Eastern diamond rattlesnake: the heaviest venomous snake in the Americas

Eastern brown snake: the second-most venomous land snake, which lives in Australia

Inland taipan: the world's most venomous land snake, which also lives in Australia

Constrictors kill by **suffocation**. These snakes include pythons, boas and anacondas. Reticulated pythons can kill and swallow prey up to the size of a pig. There are known cases of constrictors attacking or killing humans.

The reticulated python is the world's longest snake.

Croc attack!

One of the most dangerous animals in Africa is an armour-plated reptile, the Nile crocodile. It is five metres or more long. Its weapons include a powerful tail, 64 to 68 teeth and jaws with massive bite power.

The crocodile can lie as still as a log for hours on end. Then in a flash it launches a devastating attack. It normally eats fish or birds, but it can kill large animals, too. Sometimes, it seizes people near river banks, and pulls them under the water to drown and eat them.

The Nile crocodile has night vision and an excellent sense of smell – keep well away!

Holy crocodile!
The ancient Egyptians worshipped a crocodile god called Sobek (left). They believed he would protect them from attack by crocodiles along the River Nile. They even made crocodiles into mummies when they died.

The saltwater crocodile lives in rivers, but also travels far out to sea.

The biggest snapper of all is the saltwater crocodile of Australia, Southeast Asia and eastern India. It can grow up to six metres long and weigh up to 1,300 kilograms.

Tooth, tusk and claw

Many **mammals** have teeth, horns or claws, which they use to defend themselves or attack their prey.

A headlong charge by a wild animal can be terrifying. In Africa the danger may come from a Cape buffalo, which has huge, curved horns, or from an angry male elephant with long tusks. The heavyweight hippopotamus, which has huge front teeth, will attack humans, overturn boats and rampage along river banks at night.

The hippo's gaping jaws reveal long, sharp teeth.

Big cats such as lions, leopards and tigers can be dangerous company even in captivity. They can attack and kill. They do not normally prey upon humans, but a few do become 'man-eaters', especially if they are injured or short of food.

The brown bears and polar bears of the north are powerful, and will swipe and slash with their claws. They are most dangerous to us if they are disturbed when looking after their young, or are hungry.

Lions and bears are top hunters in their own environments.

From a safe distance
National parks and game reserves have strict safety rules. They allow people to view dangerous animals in safety. From a distance, we can respect their strength, and admire their beauty.

Spreaders of disease

What are the most dangerous animals of all – snakes, tigers, bears or hippos? None of these. The biggest killers are small creatures such as houseflies, mosquitoes and fleas, which pass on deadly diseases.

The housefly spreads germs wherever it feeds. It lays its eggs in human and animal waste, and in rubbish. It picks up all sorts of deadly diseases, which it can pass on to humans.

Mosquitoes are blood-suckers and their bites are very itchy. The bites themselves are not actually dangerous, but the females of some **tropical** mosquito species can pass on terrible illnesses when they bite.

The mosquito sucks blood through long, needle-like mouthparts, called the proboscis.

One of the worst illnesses that mosquitoes carry is malaria. It is caused by a **parasite**, which is passed on by mosquitoes when they bite. About 250 million people catch malaria every year and about 800,000 people die from it. Doctors and scientists around the world work hard to reduce the number of deaths from malaria, and they are developing a **vaccine**.

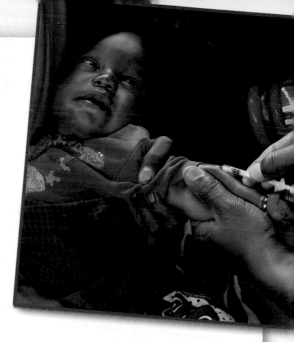

This baby is being vaccinated against yellow fever, another dangerous disease carried by mosquitoes.

The Black Death

Rats and their fleas may pass on a terrible germ to humans. It causes an illness called the bubonic plague. More than 650 years ago a plague called the Black Death raged through Asia and Europe. In Europe it killed about 75 million people.

rat flea

Quakes and waves

There is a moment of silence and then a roar and a shake. Roads crack, the ground slopes and buildings tumble. Water and gas pipes break open. There may be floods or fires. An earthquake is taking place.

In 2010 a terrible earthquake devastated Haiti. About 316,000 people died.

Earthquakes are caused by sections of the Earth's **crust** shoving against each other. Powerful shock waves spread out under the ground. People can be buried under rubble or **landslides**. The worst quakes may kill thousands of people.

The shocks from a big earthquake can force water to rush through the ocean. This movement slows down and swells into a wall of water. The sea is sucked out from the beaches and a giant wave called a tsunami crashes over the coast. In 2004 one tsunami in the Indian Ocean killed more than 230,000 people.

Scientists know where earthquakes happen, but we are never quite sure when to expect one. What people can do is design buildings to survive the shaking. They can set up a warning system for tsunamis, and practise what to do in an emergency.

A big tsunami rolls inland, destroying harbours, ships, buildings and roads.

These Japanese children wear head protection in an earthquake drill.

An angry god

The ancient Greeks believed that quakes were caused by Poseidon, the god of earthquakes, oceans and floods. When he stamped, the whole Earth shook!

Volcano blast

Humans face many dangers from the natural world. The most spectacular of these is the fiery **eruption** of a big volcano. Volcanoes are caused by the same violent forces, deep inside the Earth, that cause earthquakes.

As pressure builds, stinking gases are forced through cracks in the Earth's surface. Red-hot molten rock called lava bursts out through a volcano. The mountain can then blast apart in an eruption. This leaves a gaping **crater** and sends rocks, sparks and ash high into the sky. Streams of red-hot lava roll down the mountainside.

Lava flows over the rocks on the Pacific island of Hawaii.

The eruption of Mount Pinatubo in the Philippines in 1991 killed more than 800 people and destroyed more than 8,000 houses.

Towns can be burnt by the heat and poisoned by gas, or buried under ash and stones. The people living there may be choked to death, burnt or buried. Clouds of ash block out the sun.

People live near volcanoes because the soil is good for farming, but they take a big risk. Eruptions are tricky to forecast. If they begin slowly, there may be time to take people away from the area, and save many lives. Barriers can be built to send lava in a different direction.

The power of an eruption is massive and terrifying.

Fearsome fireworks
Sometimes a cloud of gas and rock races down a volcano at 700 kilometres per hour. It can be over 1,000°C in temperature!

Storm and wind

A building can be set on fire if lightning strikes it.

Storms threaten human life. Lightning strikes cause about 24,000 deaths each year, although few are direct hits. High winds bring trees and branches crashing down.

Extreme storms with very strong winds begin in tropical ocean areas. These storms are called hurricanes, cyclones or typhoons. They move across the Earth, wheeling around a calm centre called the eye. They bring lashings of rain. Wind speeds can reach more than 250 kilometres per hour. They whip up high waves at sea and can cause shipwrecks.

When hurricanes reach coasts and islands, the winds may rip up trees, blow off roofs, destroy houses and crops, and overturn cars.

Tornadoes or 'twisters' are terrifying whirlwinds. They form in storm clouds, creating a funnel of dust about 100 metres wide. The wind rips across the land, spinning at speeds of up to 480 kilometres per hour. They can be powerful enough to lift a train.

Storms can be forecast by weather scientists called meteorologists. They broadcast warnings on radio and television. The emergency services get ready for action. In areas where tropical storms are common, there are special buildings where people can take shelter.

Flood warning

Floods can happen after very heavy rains, when river banks crumble and are washed away. Homes fill with mud and swirling water. In the street, the water rises higher and higher, so that only boats can be used to travel. People try to escape from upstairs windows, or they cling to the roof. Floods also happen when storms drive the sea over low-lying coasts.

The first danger to humans comes from drowning in fast torrents of water. Other dangers soon follow. The floods may destroy crops and damage supplies of food. Buildings may become dangerous. Flooded drains and **sewers** may spread disease.

A family escapes by raft from flooding in Bangladesh.

Double danger!
Floods also affect wildlife. During floods in Australia in 2011, frogs and mice invaded many flooded homes. They were followed by venomous snakes.

A river burst through a broken levee in the city of New Orleans after Hurricane Katrina. Rescue boats travelled down flooded streets.

People build defences against floods. They dig ditches for drainage and raise high barriers of earth and stone, such as dykes, **levees** or sea walls. They build dams to control the flow of rivers. These bring safety, but if they break there may be a disastrous deluge. This happened in 2005 in New Orleans, USA, and more than 1,800 people died.

Large numbers of people may have to be rescued by helicopter.

Snow and ice

We all like skating, snowballing and tobogganing, but extremely cold weather brings many dangers, too. Ice makes pavements or roads treacherous to travel on and it's easy for accidents to happen.

Blizzards are big snowstorms with high winds. The wind piles up snow into huge drifts, burying cars. Heavy snow settles on roofs and can make them collapse. The weight of extra snow on a mountainside can cause an avalanche, a massive slide of snow that buries everything in its path.

Beep for safety!
Skiers and winter sports enthusiasts enjoy all the thrills of ice and snow, but they too must be well prepared. Carrying an electronic **beacon** or 'beeper' helps rescue teams find them if there is an avalanche.

The human body can be dangerously chilled by wind and frost. If outer parts of the body freeze, the blood cannot flow properly. This damages the flesh, causing **frostbite**.

The human body has ways of keeping itself warm, and we can help it by wearing extra clothing, scarves, gloves and boots in cold weather. It's safest to avoid travel if blizzards are forecast.

Walkers may not see where they are going in a blizzard, and so they become lost.

The big heat

Long periods of hot and dry weather can turn the land into a terrifying danger zone. It takes only one spark to set bushes or trees ablaze. Fire can spread at high speed, fanned by wind. It can surround villages, threatening animal and human life. It may take weeks to bring a fire under control.

Clearing trees from a forest in broad corridors may prevent fires spreading. Special aircraft can drop huge amounts of water on the flames.

Black Saturday
On Saturday 7 February 2009, 400 bush fires broke out in the Australian state of Victoria. The flames were spread by strong winds. Well over 2,000 houses were burnt down. It was reported that 173 people were killed and 414 injured. This terrible day became known as Black Saturday.

Long periods of very dry weather are called droughts. Rivers and wells run dry. Crops wither and die. There is no water for cattle. Many people become hungry and thirsty. Babies may die because of lack of water and **nourishment**. **Famines** can threaten millions of lives.

Humans cannot really control the weather, but they can work to limit the effects of drought. They can plant trees, whose roots will trap moisture in the ground. They can plant tough crops that can survive on little water.

A girl in Indonesia collects precious water from a pool.

Extreme sports

We all try to protect ourselves, but danger is also important to us. We need to take risks in order to learn how to make quick decisions and take the right actions. Often we choose to put ourselves in danger. Without adrenalin we would not have that feeling of excitement.

Skydivers jumping from a plane can delay the opening of their parachutes to enjoy rushing through the air in free-fall. Cliff-divers may dive into the sea from high rocks. They have to get the timing and angle just right to avoid injury or death.

Mountain climbers enjoy solving dangerous challenges. They hang over sheer rock faces and cling to narrow ledges. Some prefer to climb without ropes or climb up frozen waterfalls!

A climber uses ice picks to get a grip on the ice of a frozen waterfall.

Head bangers

Some common sports can be dangerous, too. Boxing, wrestling, ice hockey (right), motor racing, rugby and American football can all result in serious wounds, broken limbs and head injuries. However, these sports do have rules that reduce risk.

Daredevils

Not everyone is brave, but most of us enjoy watching other people being brave and taking risks.

At the circus, we gasp as tightrope walkers tiptoe across the high wire. We cheer as men and women in spangled costumes swing and leap from a trapeze. We're amazed as acrobats climb high on each others' shoulders. We may even see sword-swallowers, fire-eaters or showmen fired from cannon. Although all performers like to play up the drama, the dangers are very real. These stunts should never be copied or tried by people who are untrained.

Mastering a trapeze needs years of practice and a fine sense of balance.

The magnificent Blondin

In 1859 the French tightrope walker Charles Blondin walked on a high wire across Niagara Falls several times – with a wheelbarrow, in a sack, with someone on his back, and blindfolded and on stilts. Once he even stopped halfway to cook an omelette!

On films and television programmes, the person who leaps from a burning car, or who jumps over a cliff, is probably not the real actor. It is a stunt man or woman. Stunt performers learn how to take extreme risks safely. They may be helped on screen by trick camera work or by computer graphics, but even so their work can be seriously dangerous.

A daredevil motorcyclist performs a trick in mid-air.

The stunt performer helps makes the action on the screen look really thrilling.

Dangerous work

Many people face danger every day because of their work. They may handle dangerous chemicals or hot metals, or operate big cutting machines. Some need special clothing for protection, such as helmets, gloves, boots, face masks or goggles.

Some people work in dangerous places. Steeplejacks climb high to repair church steeples, towers or factory chimneys. Some workers hang on platforms at the top of skyscrapers to clean windows or stonework. Engineers and builders often work high on the top of bridges.

These construction workers are building the roof of a 348-metre skyscraper in Hong Kong.

In 2010, 33 miners in Chile were rescued after being trapped underground for 69 days.

Miners risk being trapped in deep underground shafts, or killed by floods, gas explosions or landslides. Fishing crews have one of the most dangerous jobs of all, working in storms at sea on slippery decks.

On top of the world
The world's tallest building is the Burj Khalifa in Dubai. It is 828 metres high. It has built-in units that workers can use to clean the windows safely, but the top of the tower can be reached only by ropes.

Emergency!

Accidents and disasters are dangerous for the victims. They are also dangerous for the emergency services that come to rescue them. These people risk their lives to save others.

Reach for the phone!

Emergency medical services are on call 24 hours a day to deal with accidents. The chief emergency services can be reached by calling special telephone numbers. Some well-known emergency numbers are 000 in Australia, 112 in Europe, 911 in the USA and 999 in the UK.

Firefighters battle with house fires and factory blazes, and also make sure that buildings are safe from fire. They may have to deal with a dangerous chemical spillage, or rescue people from crashed vehicles.

Firefighters carry a hose that releases a high-pressured jet of water to put out the flames.

The job of the police is to keep the public safe. They take control at accidents or disasters. They may face violent criminals, who sometimes carry knives or guns.

A lifeboat crew powers its way to a rescue.

Coastguards take action if there are accidents at sea. Lifeboat crews battle giant waves to search for sinking ships and to rescue the crews. They work closely with the helicopters of air-sea rescue.

Other rescue teams may specialize in rescue from mines or caves, from mountainsides or from the rubble of a major earthquake.

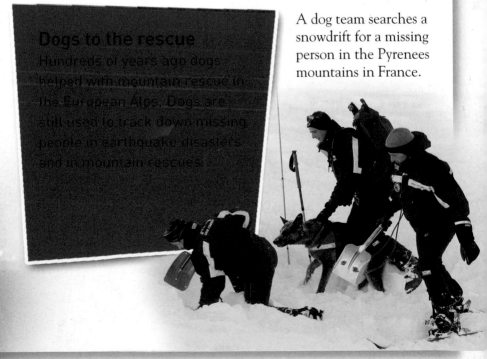

Dogs to the rescue
Hundreds of years ago dogs helped with mountain rescue in the European Alps. Dogs are still used to track down missing people in earthquake disasters and in mountain rescues.

A dog team searches a snowdrift for a missing person in the Pyrenees mountains in France.

Living with danger

An aeroplane has to make an emergency landing. A racing driver reaches a speed of more than 300 kilometres per hour. Anyone would be frightened in such dangerous situations. Fear is the most sensible reaction. It helps us to imagine what may go wrong. It helps us avoid danger.

A pilot is trained to land an aircraft safely.

Surfers take time to learn their skills. They may face dangers from riptides, massive waves, collisions from rocks, reefs or sharks. Once they can deal with such problems, they can reduce the danger levels and make the most of the thrills.

We all have to live with dangers, whether they are big or small, exciting or scary, common or unusual. The more we learn how to deal with them, the better we understand ourselves and the world around us. We learn how to protect other people in trouble, too. We learn to make the world a safer place – but perhaps not so safe that we have no fun!

Road safety is often our first lesson in coping with danger.

We can enjoy risks if we learn to be confident but careful at an early age.

Glossary

allergic Reacting badly to a particular chemical or food.

antivenom A liquid that can be injected to treat venomous bites or stings.

barbed Pointed like a fish hook. A small, angled hook that is hard to pull out of something, such as skin.

beacon Anything used for signalling or showing the way, such as a fire, a lighthouse or a radio transmitter.

chemical Another word for a substance.

crater The large, bowl-shaped opening at the top of a volcano.

crust The layer of rock that makes up the Earth's surface.

eruption The blast from a volcano. An eruption may include gases, rocks, lava (molten rock) and ash.

famine An extreme shortage of food that causes widespread starvation.

frostbite Damage to the flesh caused by the freezing of the body.

germ A tiny living organism that can make a person ill.

gland One of the small organs in the body that produces chemicals to make the body work properly.

landslide The slip downwards, such as down a mountainside, of a large amount of soil or rock.

levee In America, a natural or purpose-built river bank that holds back floods.

mammal An animal that has hair and which feeds its young on milk from its body.

nerves Fibres that carry messages between the brain and other parts of the body.

nourishment Food that is good for keeping the body alive.

parasite An animal that lives on or in another animal.

prey An animal that is hunted and eaten by another animal.

sewer A large drain that carries off waste and foul water.

species A group of plants or animals that breed together to produce young.

starvation Extreme hunger that puts life at risk.

suffocation Causing an animal's death by preventing it from breathing.

swarm A large group of insects that has gathered together to feed or breed.

tropical Living in the warm and wet countries near the Equator.

venom The poison produced by some animals that bite and sting.

vaccine A small amount of a virus that is injected into the body to build up defences against a particular disease.

vessel Any of the tubes that carry blood through the body.

Index

avalanches 32

bears 21, 22
bees 14
Black Death 23
blizzards 32, 33

circus acts 38
crocodiles 18–19

deathcap mushrooms 9
droughts 35

earthquakes 4, 24–25,
  26, 43
elephants 20

fires 24, 28, 34, 42
fleas 22, 23
floods 4, 24, 25, 30–31, 41
frostbite 33, 46

germs 7, 22, 23, 46

hippopotamuses 20, 22
houseflies 22
hurricanes 28, 31

jellyfish 11

landslides 24, 41, 46
lightning 28
lions 21

locusts 15

malaria 23
mines 41, 43
mosquitoes 22, 23

poisonous plants 4, 8–9

rats 23

scorpions 12, 13
sharks 10–11, 44
snakes 16–17, 22, 30
snow 32–33, 43
spiders 12, 13
sports 4, 5, 36–37, 44
storms 28–29, 30, 41
stunts 38, 39

tigers 4, 21, 22
tornadoes 29
tsunamis 25
  see also waves

venom 11, 12, 13, 14, 16,
  17, 47
volcanoes 26–27

wasps 14, 15
waves 25, 28, 43, 44
winds 28–29, 32, 33, 34